Pumpkins

T0349869

HEINLE
CENGAGE Learning™

Y|S|G
A YBM COMPANY

Young & Son
Global, Inc.

Contents

seeds

sprout

vine

leaves

flower

pumpkin

Do you like pumpkin pie?
Pumpkin pie is made from pumpkins.
How does a pumpkin grow?

First, pumpkins begin as seeds.
You plant pumpkin seeds.
The seeds are flat.

Next, the seed grows into a sprout.
The sprout is small.

leaves

vine

Then, the sprout grows into a vine with leaves.
The vine is long.

Next, the vine grows flowers.
The flowers are yellow.

Then, the flowers grow into pumpkins.
The pumpkins are green.

The green pumpkins grow big.

They turn orange.

Now, the pumpkins are ready to pick.

Life Cycle of a Pumpkin

seed

sprout

vine

flower

green pumpkin

orange pumpkin

There are many seeds inside the pumpkins.
The seeds will grow into new plants.

How does a pumpkin grow?

Seeds to Pumpkins

I plant a pumpkin seed.
I plant a pumpkin seed.
A vine grows along the ground,
Yellow flowers, too.

My pumpkin is small.
My pumpkin is small.
It will grow big and orange,
Then I'll take it home.

Index